T0196369

JESUS WAS NOT CRUCIFIED WHEN AS HAS BEEN TAUGHT

Easter Is Not When Jesus Was Resurrected

Apostle Frederick E. Franklin

authorHOUSE®

AuthorHouse™
1663 Liberty Drive
Bloomington, IN 47403
www.authorhouse.com
Phone: 1-800-839-8640

Published by AuthorHouse 10/16/2013

ISBN: 978-1-4918-2781-9 (sc)
ISBN: 978-1-4918-2780-2 (e)

Library of Congress Control Number: 2013918782

Any people depicted in stock imagery provided by Thinkstock are
models, and such images are being used for illustrative purposes only.
Certain stock imagery © Thinkstock.

This book is printed on acid-free paper.

INTRODUCTION

We write this short book to correct the errors that have been taught and believed about JESUS of Nazareth's death, burial and resurrection. Your confusion related to what has been taught should be considerable.

After reading this book, you will never look at the teachings concerning Easter and JESUS' Death and Resurrection the same again. As the Title indicates, Easter is not JESUS's Resurrection.

JESUS WAS NOT CRUCIFIED WHEN AS HAS BEEN TAUGHT

Most Christians and so-called Christians will tell you Jesus Christ of Nazareth, the Son of God, was crucified on a Friday and rose on Sunday morning. They say this in spite of the Bible saying that he was in the grave three days and three nights. What they say then is a lie. There is no way that there are three days and three nights between Friday and early Sunday morning. The Bible clearly states that Jesus was crucified and died 3:00 p.m. in the afternoon.

Mark, Ch. 15, Vs. 25, 33 & 37

"And it was the third hour, and they crucified him. And when the 6th hours was come, there was darkness over the whole land until the ninth hour. And Jesus cried with a loud voice, and gave up the ghost."

1

The third hour is 9:00 a.m., the sixth hour is 12:00 p.m. (noon) and the ninth hour is 3:00 p.m.

The Bible says that Jesus rose from the dead on the first day of the week when it was yet dark.

<u>John, Ch. 20, Vs. 1,16 & 17</u>
"The first day of the week cometh Mary Magdalene early, when it was yet dark, unto the sepulcher, and seeth the stone taken away from the sepulcher. Jesus saith unto her, Mary. She turned herself, and saith unto him, Rabboni; which is to say Master. Jesus saith unto her, Touch me not; I am not ascended to my Father; and to my God, and your God."

The above scriptures let us know that Jesus was resurrected from the dead on what we call "Sunday morning before day".

According to the lie that is being taught by nearly all the preachers, this means Jesus died on Friday afternoon at 3:00 p.m. and rose on Sunday morning before daylight. A quick count on your fingers will give you a quick and correct conclusion that this is a lie. Jesus said that He would be in the grave three days and three nights.

Matthew, Ch. 12, V. 40
"For as Jonas was three days and three nights in the whale's belly; so shall the Son be three days and three nights in the heart of the earth."

John Ch. 2, V. 19
"Jesus answered and said unto them, Destroy this temple, and in three days I will raise it up."

There is no way that you can get three days and three nights between Friday afternoon at 3:00 p.m. and Sunday before daylight. You might then wonder, where did those preachers of the lie get Friday as the day Jesus was crucified. Well, they came to this Friday lie by two means. Number 1: The Pope in 325 A.D. birth this lie to get people to celebrate the resurrection on Easter, which was the worship of the pagan Spring goddess. This Friday is that Friday before the worship of the Spring goddess that the Pope declared there should be no eating of meat except fish.

It was written and preached by a former Catholic, that in his extensive research of the origins of Catholic Church doctrine, the eating only of fish meat on Friday was a creation of the Pope around 325 A.D. He wrote that the Pope made this decree to help the fishing merchants, to gain their support. To say JESUS died on Friday could help enhance participation in this dedicated fish day.

Number 2: Misunderstanding the scriptures is the other reason why people have held to Friday as being when Jesus died. The Bible says that Jesus died before the Sabbath. It was therefore assumed to them that the Sabbath was referring to the seventh day of the week which people say is Saturday, thereby, concluding that Friday had to be when Jesus was crucified.

There is much error in the above assumption and conclusion. The scriptures did say that

Jesus died on the day before the Sabbath, but it was a high Sabbath and not the weekly Sabbath day, not the seventh day.

Mark, Ch. 15, Vs. 42, 43 & 46

"And now when the evening was come it was time for preparation, that is the day before the Sabbath, Joseph of Arimathaea, an honorable counselor, which also waited for the Kingdom of God, came, and went in boldly unto Pilate, and craved the body of Jesus. And he bought fine linen, and took him down, and wrapped him in the linen, and laid him in the sepulcher which was hewn out of rocks, and rolled the stone unto the door of the sepulcher."

John, Ch. 19, V. 31

"The Jews, therefore, because it was the preparation, that the bodies should not remain upon the cross on the sabbath day (for that sabbath day was an high day) . . ."

The word sabbath means a time to cease or rest from work. There were several days that God told the children of Israel to observe/celebrate that he told them not to work on those particular days or high sabbaths. These were the high days or high Sabbaths.

The Jew's special days of observance, such as feast days, were called high sabbath days. God had told Moses and Israel to always observe the Passover. The Passover was the time that the first born of Egypt was slain at the same time that those of Israel that put lamb's blood on certain specified places of their house were spared/passed over. This killing of a lamb and using his blood to protect and deliver God's people was a picture of what Jesus crucifying did in saving us that would be saved. This was the last plague upon Egypt by God that was necessary for Pharaoh to allow the children of Israel to be freed from slavery. The observance of this time was called the Passover and a high sabbath. This was the first month of the year and the (14) fourteenth day, as declared by God. Therefore, this Passover would always be on the same day of the month, unlike Easter, the day of the worship of the Spring goddess which appears on different days of March and April.

<u>Exodus, Ch. 11, Vs. 4 & 5</u>
"And Moses said, Thus saith the LORD, About midnight will I go out into the midst of Egypt: And all the first born in the land of Egypt shall die, from first born of Pharaoh that sitteth on the throne, even unto first born of the maidservants that is behind the mill, and all the first born of beasts."

<u>Exodus, Ch. 12, Vs. 5 & 6</u>
"Your Lamb shall be without blemish . . . kill it in the evening."

<u>Exodus, Ch. 12, Vs. 6, 7& 13</u>
". . . and the whole assembly of the congregation of Israel . . . shall take of the blood, and strike it on the two side posts and on the upper door of the posts of the houses, wherein they shall eat it. And the blood shall be to you a token upon the houses where ye are: and when I see the blood, I will pass over you, and the plague shall not be upon you to destroy you, when I smite the land of Egypt."

Exodus, Ch. 12, Vs. 1 & 2

"And the LORD spake unto Moses and Aaron in the land of Egypt, saying, This month shall be unto you the beginning of months: it shall be the first month of the year to you."

Exodus, Ch. 12, Vs. 5, 6 & 14

"Your lamb shall be without blemish . . . And ye shall keep it up until the fourteenth day of the same month: and the whole assembly of the congregation shall kill it in the evening. And this day shall be unto you for a memorial: and ye shall keep it a feast to the LORD throughout your generations; ye shall keep it a feast by an ordinance forever."

Deuteronomy, Ch. 16, V. 1

"Observe the month of Abib and keep the Passover unto the LORD thy God: for in the month of Abib the LORD thy God brought thee forth out of Egypt by night."

Since JESUS was indeed resurrected on the first day of the week, then there were two sabbaths between JESUS' death and resurrection. The high sabbath and the seventh day sabbath.

From the above scriptures, you can clearly see that Easter, the worship of the pagan Spring goddess, is not the day of the resurrection of JESUS Christ of Nazareth. From the above discussion and scriptures it is clear that Friday was not when JESUS was crucified. From Friday at 3:00 p.m. to Sunday morning before daylight there are not three days and three nights. Between Friday at 3:00 p.m. to Saturday 3:00 p.m. are (24) twenty-four hours. Assuming that daylight came at about 6:00 a.m. on Sunday morning; then from 3:00 p.m. Saturday to Sunday morning at 6:00 a.m. is only (15) fifteen hours. Therefore, according to the Friday Lie, JESUS was in the grave only 24 plus 15 hours which equals to 39 hours. You cannot get three days and three nights in this thirty-nine (39) hour time span.

Some have <u>correctly</u> concluded that JESUS was not crucified on Friday, but have <u>incorrectly</u> concluded that JESUS was in the grave for (72) seventy-two hours. JESUS was not raised from the dead after seventy-two hours. In fact, it was far from (72) seventy-two hours. It was only between fifty-one (51) to sixty-three (63) hours. JESUS died on the cross on the (5th) fifth day at the ninth hour. This is Thursday at 3:00 p.m.

If you assume that Jesus rose after seventy-two hours (72) hours, then that means that the scriptures have to be wrong. Either Jesus did not die at 3:00 p.m. (9th) ninth-hour or he was not resurrected before daylight on the (1st) first day, Saturday night or Sunday morning.

You must remember/understand that a day that we refer to which starts at 12:00 a.m., midnight, is not the same as what God refers to as a (24th) twenty-four hour day. The day referred to in the Bible is as God has ordained. God made the day and therefore it is what He says and not as it has been changed by men to be. God's days starts evening or dark and goes to the next beginning of evening or dark. This is as God said at the very beginning in the Holy Bible in Genesis, Chapter 1.

Genesis, Ch. 1, Vs. 3, 4 & 5

"And God said, Let there be light: and there was light. And God saw the light that it was good: and God divided the light from darkness. And God called light Day, and the darkness called he Night. <u>And the evening and the morning were the first day."</u>

Genesis, Ch. 1, V.8

And God called the firmaments Heaven. <u>And the evening and the morning were the second day</u>."

Genesis, Ch. 1, V.13

<u>And the evening and the morning were the third day</u>."

Likewise, for the fourth, fifth, sixth, and, seventh days, God says that those days begin at evening and end after the morning. The evening is all dark time and morning is all day light time.

Seventy-two hours from 6:00 a.m. would mean that Jesus had to die at 6:00 a.m. Thursday morning. If you go to the extreme of when he rose, Saturday beginning at night, assuming 6:00 p.m., then Jesus would had to die at 6:00 p.m. on Wednesday. Neither of the above (72) seventy-two hour periods can be true nor any other combination to get (72) seventy-two hours between those two extremes can be true. Remember, JESUS was buried before the sabbath.

You may think that maybe JESUS was referring to his body being in the earth three days and three nights. If this was true, then we could justify the seventy-two (72) hours by saying it was around 6:00 p.m. when his body was in the tomb. This sounds like a good argument, but it is not. JESUS said that he would be "in the heart of the earth" as Jonas was "in the whale's belly". Being in a tomb or cave does not indicate the center part or inner part of the earth as "heart" and "belly" symbolizes. The correct conclusion then is that Jesus was referring to his soul being in the heart of the earth. When JESUS died at 3:00 p.m., he, his, soul, went into the heart of the earth. This is what the Scriptures of I Peter Chapter 3 Verse 18 and 19 are referring to.

I Peter, Ch. 3, Vs.18 & 19
"For Christ also hath once suffered for sins, the just for the unjust, that he might bring us to God, being put to death in the flesh, but quickened by the Spirit: By which also he went and preached unto the spirits in prison . . ."

Jesus referring to his soul being in the heart of the earth is what is indicated to one of the men being crucified when he was crucified.

Luke, Ch. 23, Vs.42 & 43
"And he said unto Jesus, Lord, remember me when thou comest into thy Kingdom. And Jesus said unto him, Verily I say unto thee, Today shalt thou be with me in paradise."

You might argue then and say, what about when JESUS said "destroy this body" and I will raise it; this could not be referring to his soul.

John, Ch. 2, Vs. 19, 20 & 21
"Jesus answered and said unto them Destroy this temple, and in three days I will raise it up. Then said the Jews, Forty and six years was this temple building, and wilt thou rear it up

in three days? But, he spake of the temple of his body."

You are right that JESUS was talking about his body being raised from the dead in the above scripture, however, the word "in" must not be overlooked. Jesus said that he would raise his body "in" three days and three nights. The word "in" has the same usage in the above scripture as "within".

The sum of the matter is this, when Jesus said "three days and three nights" he was using it as we might say:

1. I work five days a week;
2. I work five nights a week;
3. I attend church three days a week;
4. I attend church three nights a week;
5. I go to school five days a week;
6. I got to school five nights a week;
7. I pray every day and every night of the week.

In all of the above examples what we might say, we are not saying that the day and night equals a twenty-four (24) hour period. We would only be saying that on those/that particular day(s) or night(s) we did something or something happened.

If for no other reason why JESUS was not in the heart of the earth for seventy-two (72) hour is because for it to be so, whether body or soul, he would have gone or been put there when it was night. He was resurrected at night, therefore, seventy-two hours earlier would have been night. He died at 3:00 p.m. and this is not night. Also, Joseph of Arimathaea, a rich man and one who believed in JESUS, made sure he put him in the grave before night. He made sure because night was the beginning of the high Sabbath and no dead body was allowed to be unburied during that special time.

<u>John Ch. 19, V.31</u>
"The Jews therefore, because it was the preparation, that the bodies should not remain upon the cross on the sabbath day (for that sabbath day was an high day) . . ."

Mark Ch. 15, Vs. 43 & 46

"Joseph of Arimathaea, an honorable counselor, which waited for the Kingdom of God, came and went boldly unto Pilate, and craved the body of Jesus. And he bought fine linen, and took him down and wrapped him in the linen, and laid him in a sepulcher which was hewn out of rock, and rolled the stone unto the door of the sepulcher."

We know that this was day time also because Mary Magdalene and Mary, the mother of JESUS, went and prepared after leaving the tomb, probably walking, probably some substantial amount of time, spices and ointments. They were not allowed to prepare anything when night would have begun, which would have been the high Sabbath.

Luke, Ch. 23, Vs. 55 & 56

"And the women also, which came with him from Galilee, followed after, and beheld the sepulcher, and how his body was laid. And they returned, and prepared species and ointments; and rested the Sabbath day according to the commandment."

It is very obvious then that it was daytime when Jesus was put in the grave.

We have said that JESUS was crucified and died on Thursday at 3:00 p.m. The scripture said he arose on the first day of the week when it was dark. The first day of the week when it was dark would then be Saturday night or Sunday before daylight.

In the above time frame are three days and three nights. Sunday before daylight to Saturday night is <u>one night</u>, the <u>third night.</u> Saturday daylight time is <u>one day</u>, the third day. Saturday before daylight to Friday night is <u>one night</u>, the <u>second night</u>. Friday daylight time is one day, the <u>second day</u>. Friday before daylight to Thursday night is <u>one night</u>, the <u>first night</u>. Thursday before daylight time is <u>one day</u>, the <u>first day</u>.

The above shows there are three days and three nights between 3:00 p.m. Thursday to before daylight on Sunday morning. You might say then, yes, I must agree that JESUS did not die on Friday and Easter is not when

JESUS was resurrected, but what is wrong with observing these times to give honor to JESUS? JESUS should be given honor at all times. But, God/JESUS does not share worship and glory with any one, especially a pagan god, the Spring goddess. Besides that, God only accepts undefiled worship.

<u>John, Ch. 4, V.24</u>
"God is a Spirit: and they that worship him must worship him in spirit and in truth."

There is certainly no truth in saying that JESUS died on Friday. There is no truth that Easter, the celebration of the Spring goddess, is when JESUS was resurrected from the dead. There is no truth that rabbits lay eggs as is part of the lie told to children during Easter celebrations. To think that God desires any worship to be given as a part of this idolatry is totally misguided and ungodly thinking.

<u>Matthew, Ch. 15, V. 9</u>
"But in vain they worship me, teaching for doctrines the commandments of men."

God never has expected, not remotely, his people to mix anything of worship to him with idolatry.

II Corinthians, Ch. 6, Vs. 17 & 18
Wherefore come out from among them, and be ye separate, saith the Lord, and touch not the unclean things, and I will receive you, and will be a father to you, and ye shall be my sons and daughters, saith the Lord Almighty."

The people of the world, whether they know JESUS or not, celebrate Easter. The people of the world whether they curse the name of JESUS or not, celebrate Easter. The people of the world love Easter celebration.

I John, Ch. 2, V. 15
"Love not the world, neither the thing that are in the world. If any man love the world, the love of the Father is not in him."

It is even an abomination for God's saints to eat Easter dinner and Easter eggs, candy and other such foods.

I Corinthians, Ch.10, Vs. 27 & 28

"If any of them that believe not bid you to a feast, and ye be disposed to go; whatsoever is set before you, eat, asking no questions for conscience sake. But, if any man say unto you, This is offered as sacrifice unto idols eat not for his sake that shewed it, and for conscience sake . . ."

What we have written thus far is mainly intended for those who believe that JESUS Christ of Nazareth was the Son of God and the Jews' long looked for Messiah. We, however, understand that there are Jews and others who do not believe that JESUS of Nazareth was this Messiah. They do not believe that JESUS Of Nazareth fulfilled the symbolism associated with the Passover. One of the main criticisms is that JESUS was not killed in the evening, as the scriptures said when the Passover lamb must be killed.

Exodus, Ch. 12, V.6

"And ye shall keep it up until the fourteenth day of the same month: and the whole assembly of the congregation of Israel shall <u>kill it in the evening</u>."

The Pharisees, Scribes and other Jews that plotted against JESUS was well aware that if Jesus was to be the Messiah and that slain lamb associated with the Passover, then he would have to die in the evening. That is why they worked so diligently, starting early in the morning and the evening before to get JESUS crucified and to die other than the evening. So, they started the crucifixion at 9:00 a.m. knowing that he had to die in the daylight hours and not evening.

None of this plotting would catch God by surprise. But you might say, but he died at 3:00 p.m. Yes, we agree. That is why God caused darkness on the earth starting at noon until Jesus finally died at 3:00 p.m.

<u>Luke, Ch. 23, Vs. 44, 45 & 46</u>
"And it was about the sixth hour, and there was darkness over all the earth until the ninth hour. And the sun was darkened, and the veil of the temple was rented in the midst. And

when Jesus had cried with a loud voice, he said, Father into thy hands I commend my spirit: and having said thus, he gave up the ghost."

Mark, Ch. 15, Vs. 1, 25, 33, 34 & 37

"And straightway in the morning the chief priests held consultation with the elders and scribes and the whole council, and bond Jesus and carried him away, and delivered him to Pilate. And it was the third hour and they crucified him. And when the sixth hour was come, there was darkness over the whole land until the ninth hour, Jesus cried with a loud voice, saying Eloi Eloi, lama sabachthani? which is being interpreted, My God, my God, why hast thou forsaken me? And Jesus cried with a loud voice, and gave up the ghost."

So you see, it was dark just as evening time when JESUS died. Evening is defined by darkness. Thus, fulfilling the scriptures, JESUS the slain lamb died in darkness as did the Passover lamb.

So you might ask then, why was not JESUS then killed at the beginning of the Passover as was the Passover Lamb? Answer that if you can, you might ask? Well, we will. The Passover began the evening before JESUS died. Since JESUS died at 3:00 p.m., the (9th) nineth hour, then JESUS died about (21) twenty-one hours after the Passover had begun. The reason this happened is because of what happened during Joshua time. During that time, Joshua and the children of Israel were in a great battle against the Amorites. At this time Joshua prayed to God to allow the Sun not to set before he and Israel could win the battle. God answered the prayer of Joshua and the Sun did not set about a whole day. This was about (21) twenty-one hours. So God made the adjustment with the Passover, JESUS' death, to allow for this delayed time. This shows the importance of JESUS' death. The whole universe had to acknowledge it. It was no little thing. That shows how much God cares about mankind.

Joshua Ch. 10, Vs. 12 & 13

"Then spake Joshua to the LORD in the day when the LORD delivered up the Amorites before the children of Israel, and he said in the sight of Israel, Sun, stand thou still upon Gibeon and thou Moon, in the valley of Ajalon. And the sun stood still, and the moon stayed, until the people avenged themselves upon their enemies. Is not this written in the book of Jasher? So the sun stood still in the midst of heaven, and hasted not to go down about a whole day."

Don't you know that after all of this, that it is an abomination to try and change JESUS' resurrection to a pagan holiday; the abominable Easter.

God had the universe to take note of the death of JESUS. Yet, the Catholic Church, has decreed that the death of JESUS is to be changed to align up with some mythical goddess. To align up with the lie of a Spring goddess. The lie of a goddess of Viginity. To align up with the lie of when this goddess gave birth to their mythical god. To align up with when this lie of a Spring goddess that gave birth to their top god, the Sun god. This Spring goddess was called Athena, the Roman goddess. The Greeks had their own Spring goddess called Diana. The lie was that Athena gave birth as a virgin to Zeus. The lie was that Diana gave birth as a virgin to Apollo.

Apostle Paul of the Holy Scriptures/Bible of the New Testament had to deal with this this lie of Diana when he visited the City of Ephesus. That heathen City was in total embrace of this Diana lie.

<u>Acts Ch. 19, Vs. 24-34</u>
"For a certain man named Demetrius, a silversmith, which made silver shrines for Diana, brought no small gain unto the craftsmen; Whom he called together with the workmen of like occupation, and said, Sirs, ye know that by this craft we have our wealth. Moreover ye see and hear, that not alone at Ephesus, but almost throughout all Asia, Paul hath persuaded and turned away much people, saying that they be no gods, which are made by hands: So that not only our craft

is in danger to be set at nought but also that the temple of the great goddess Diana should be despised, and her magnificence should be destroyed, whom all Asia and the world worshippeth. And when they heard these sayings, they were full of wrath, and cried out, saying, Great is Diana of the Ephesians. And the whole city was filled with confusion: and having caught Gaius and Aristarchus, men of Macedonia, Paul's companions in travel, they rushed with one accord into the theatre. And when Paul would have entered in unto the people, the disciples suffered him not. And certain of the chief of Asia, which were his friends, sent unto him, desiring him that he would not adventure himself into the theatre. Some therefore cried one thing, and some another: for the assembly was confused; and the more part knew not wherefore they were come together. And they drew Alexander out of the multitude, the Jews putting him forward. And Alexander beckoned with the hand, and would have made his defence unto the people. But when they knew that he was a Jew, all with one voice about the space of two hours cried out, Great is Diana of the Ephesians."

As we mentioned earlier, the birth of this Easter lie as the resurrection of JESUS was established in 325 A.D. In the 325 A.D. Council of Nicean, the Pope of the Catholic Church during that time came in agreement with Constantine, the Emperor of Rome, for that Church to come together with Rome as one. Part of this alliance was that the Pope agreed with Constantine to tell the lie that JESUS was resurrected from the dead at the same time as the celebration of Easter. Easter was a day set aside to celebrate the Spring goddess. This consent and alliance is why the Catholic Church put so much emphasis on the worship of the virgin Mary, the mother of JESUS. In fact, the Catholic Church put more emphasis on the virgin Mary than on JESUS. Mary whom gave birth in the flesh as a virgin to JESUS, the God of the universe.

As Apostle Paul had to contend with the lie of Easter in his day, we likewise in this day have to contend with this Easter lie. During the time after the 325 A.D. Council of Nicean, the Catholic Church killed off all the true saints/ followers of JESUS who would not accept the Easter celebration of JESUS' Resurrection.

Since the killing off of God's true saints/ followers, nearly all of the so-called Christian world celebrates Easter. Now in these last days, the end times, through this Book and through other of our writings, God is bring the truth of JESUS' Resurrection back to the earth. God is revealing that it is a lie that Easter was the Resurrection of JESUS of Nazareth.

We end with these words from God. If you continue in the idolatry of Easter, when you die, you will go to hell and the lake of fire where you will burn day and night for ever and evermore.

APOSTLE FREDERICK E. FRANKLIN'S TESTIMONY

Let me give you my personal testimony. Let me tell you about how I got filled with the Holy Ghost. Back in 1985 I lived in Washington, D.C. I was not married at that time. It was in October of 1985. I had my own business as a Utilities Engineering Consultant. As a sinner and as usually was the case, I left out of a certain bar around 1:00 am. When finally I reached the place where I was living and was opening my door, the telephone began to ring. I went in and answered the telephone. It was my first cousin calling from Mobile, Alabama. He, also, was about high and was just getting in from a bar. As usually was the case, we started talking about God. We knew little to nothing about God, but somehow we always started talking about God. As we talked, I started talking about the preachers of God. I said that those O lying preachers that say they lay hands on people and they get healed are the worst ones. I said only Jesus could heal someone like that. I at least knew that Jesus could heal like that. My cousin said you are right. Two drunks talking. He then said the only other ones who could do that were Peter, John, Paul and the other Apostles of the Holy Bible. I was shocked. I was so shocked that I got sober. I said what! What! He said yes! Peter, John, Paul and the other Apostles laid hands on the people and they got healed. I was totally astounded! I was totally amazed! I was sober!

After we hanged up the telephone, I went and picked up the Bible which I had kept with me since about 1963. I had never opened the Bible I was just religious and kept it with me. I had been putting off reading it for all these years. When the urge would come to me to read it, I would put it off to the next month, or next week, or next day, or when I finished a certain project, or when I finished during this or that. I did not know it then, but I know now, the urge was God trying to get me to read the Bible. I finally dusted off and opened that Bible. It was now around 2:00 am. I wanted to see for myself where it said that a man could lay hands on a person and he or she could get healed. I was after all, an Electrical Engineer and this was illogical. How could flesh, blood and bones heal someone? It did not make any sense. Not having any idea where to look, I searched and searched and searched. I read and read and read. Finally, somewhere between 3:00-4:00 am, I found it. I saw that Peter laid hands on people and they got healed. It was amazing! It was like a very bright light was turned on in my head. I was speechless. To understand the greatness of my astonishment, you need to understand my childhood hopelessness. I, as a child, being black brought up in Alabama, living far out in a rural area, started working when I was four years old. I would go outside of our house at night, walking through the woods, looking up in the sky at the moon and the stars, and ask God why? I knew it had to be a God. I would ask God why would he leave his children down on this earth at the mercy of Satan? Satan of course, I knew, had no mercy. I could not understand why. Everything that seemed to be good, appeared to be on Satan's side. The evil people had it. White folks had it who were doing evil. Why, why, why, was my question? I never received an answer. It appeared that God could care less about the suffering of and in justice to his children on this earth.

When I saw that someone could get healed by another just by laying hands on them, then I understood clearly the answer to my why. I understood that God had not left us at the mercy of Satan. I, however, wanted to see could anyone lay hands on people and they could get healed. As I continued to search and read, now about day break, I "discovered" that you had to have the Holy Ghost to be able to heal. I wanted then to see could anyone receive the Holy Ghost. Now far in the morning of the next day, I "discovered" that anyone could receive the Holy Ghost. I "discovered" that you spoke in tongues when you received the Holy Ghost. My life desire would never be the same again. I wanted to see how I could receive the Holy Ghost. I learned that you had to repent. So, I asked God to forgive my sins. Then I asked God to give me the Holy Ghost, let me speak in tongues. Nothing happened. I did not speak in tongues. All that day I was asking God to forgive my sins and to let me speak in tongues. I did not work that day. This went on all day and into the night. Nothing ever happened. Exhausted I fell asleep into the next morning. When I woke the next day I started doing the same thing. I asked God to forgive my sins and let me speak in tongues. Nothing happened. I thought that maybe I need to read God's word and then I might receive the Holy Ghost. So, I read several Books of the Bible. Then I asked God to forgive my sins and let me speak in tongues. Nothing happened. I did this over and over each day and nothing ever happened. I had stop working all together. To receive the Holy Ghost was the most important thing in my life. I made a pledge to God that I would not go to the bars again. Nothing happened as I sought for the Holy Ghost. I made a pledge to God to stop drinking and stop smoking marijuana. Nothing happened. I made a pledge to God to stop fornicating. Nothing happened as I sought for the Holy Ghost. I was praying for the Holy Ghost and reading God's word and nothing happened. I decided to read the whole Bible. I read from Genesis through the Book of Revelation and nothing happened as I sought for the Holy Ghost during that time. Now it was the end of the year of 1985 and nothing happened as I sought for the Holy Ghost. I decided to move from Washington, D.C., back to my house in Montgomery, Alabama. Now after reading the whole Bible, I was praying about (22) twenty two hours a day to receive the Holy Ghost and nothing happened. I started crying and praying and nothing happened. I had only cried (4) four times in my life. I remember all the way back from (2) two years old. Crying and seeking for the Holy Ghost is all I did. I never spoke in tongues. This crying and seeking God for the Holy Ghost reached now into August of the year 1986. I had counted all of the months, weeks, and days to that time of seeking for the Holy Ghost, now seeking about (22) twenty two hours a day. I had about (3) three months before, cleaned out my house of everything that I thought was sinful. I threw away all pornography, whiskey, wine and beer, marijuana and whatever I thought was sinful into my trash can. I did this and nothing ever happened. Now here it was in August, seeking to speak in tongues and I had not. I said, I thought, that maybe I need to join a Church. This might would help, I thought. I looked into the yellow pages of the phone book and chose (4) four churches that I would check out to join. This was now August 3, 1986. I was still seeking God for the Holy Ghost. I still was crying and praying to speak in tongues about (22) twenty two hours a day. On August 3, 1986, I turned on my television early in the morning and turning the channels I saw and heard some ridiculous sounding Church Choir singing with the TV camera shaking. I stopped to see what in the world would this be on television so unprofessional. I was amazed. I had once worked at a television station in Cleveland, Ohio, and I was just amazed at this. As I looked and listened in amazement, a young woman came before the camera to introduce/present her Apostle. She said that her Apostle laid hands on people, preformed many miracles and prayed for many to receive the Holy Ghost. This really caught my attention. I thought, could this be the answer to my quest? Then her Apostle came forth. A black, tall, old man, Apostle William A. Tumlin. I had already decided that I wanted to join a church under an old man who really knew something about

God. Also, I wanted it to be a small church. I did not want anything to be like that Baptist Church that I was brought up in. All they cared about was looks, a big choir, a big church, a big funeral, always looks. They cared about looks, but yet certain ones was committing adultery and it seemed to be alright. Many were drunks and it seemed not to matter. I was brought up in this and had not learned hardly anything that I had finally read in the Bible.

Yet seeking God for the Holy Ghost, on August 10, 1986, I decided to first check out this Church and Apostle that I had seen on Television, before checking out the other churches. I went to the Church and it was a small church. I went into the Church and the Apostle preached and ask did anyone want to join the Church, I to my amazement went up and join the Church. I thought that the Apostle would pray for me to receive the Holy Ghost, but he did not. I was confused. After the service was dismissed, I went to the Apostle's wife and told her that I wanted to receive the Holy Ghost. She said, Oh, I thought you already had the Holy Ghost. She told me to go and tell the Apostle. I went to the Apostle and said I want to receive the Holy Ghost. He said Oh, I thought you already had the Holy Ghost. He said come back, either next Sunday or that afternoon before the 6:00 taping of the radio broadcast, and he would pray for me to receive the Holy Ghost. I said that I would come back before the taping of the broadcast. I was not about to wait for a whole week. I could tell you how many months, weeks and days I had been seeking for the Holy Ghost. I had been seeking for the Holy Ghost every day since October of 1985 and it was now August 10, 1986.

When I went home from Apostle Tumlin's Church, The All Nations Church of God, I did something that was key to me receiving the Holy Ghost. Remember I told you that I threw away all, pornography, whiskey, wine, beer, marijuana and other things I thought was sinful into my trash can. Well, I went back to my trash can and I got (2) two marijuana joints out of it and brought them back into my house. I had stop smoking marijuana during my time of seeking the Holy Ghost and had no intentions of smoking anymore. I did not know it at that time, but I know it now, it was Satan that convinced me to get those (2) two joints out of my trash can. I thought, Satan told me, that I might need them if I got a headache. I just had them in my closet in case I might need them for a headache. The Devil, Satan, just made a fool out of me. The only time I had those headaches is when I had a hangover. I was not going to have a hangover because I had stop drinking. What a fool. However, on August, 10, 1986, before I went back to receive the Holy Ghost, it had to be God who told me, I went to my closet and got those two joints and flushed them down my toilet stool. When I did this, it felt like a very, very, heavy weight was taken off me. At 5:00 on August 10, 1986, I was back at Apostle Tumlin's Church, The All Nations Church of God, to receive the Holy Ghost. I went in the Church and sat down in about the fourth row of the pews, next to the aisle, on the left side looking from the pulpit. There were about (3) three to (4) four people in the sanctuary, including the Apostle's wife. They were there praying. However, the Apostle was nowhere to be seen. I sat there waiting for the Apostle and he never showed up. It was now 5:30 pm and there was no sign of the Apostle. I was getting very anxious because the radio broadcast's taping was to start at 6:00 pm. Finally, the Apostle came out of a room from the front of the Church. I was so excited! I finally was going to receive the Holy Ghost! The Apostle walked towards me and down the aisle and right by me and went into the rest room near the entrance to the Church. He did not say one word to me. Not even a gesture toward me. Some minutes past by and he was still back there. I just kept praying. I just kept repenting. Finally he came out. He came to the back of me and put his hands on my head and said receive the Holy Ghost. I was excited and nervous. I did not know what to expect. Then with his hands on my head, he said speak in tongues. I said to myself, what is this man talking about? I said to myself, you have to receive the Holy Ghost before you speak in tongues. He, the Apostle, just kept saying speak in tongues. Then he, with hands on my head, started speaking in tongues. Then he said receive the Holy Ghost, speak in tongues. Then he started speaking in tongues. Then he said speak in tongues with his hands on my head. Then to my amazement he began to give up on me and remove his hands, I stood up so his hands could not be removed. I thought to myself, no, no, you are not going to give up on me this quick. So he let his hands stay on my head and began to speak in tongues. Then he said speak in tongues. I by this time, with the Apostle's hands on my head, was standing in front of the church facing the pews, but I did not know it. He said again speak in tongues. I said to myself this is not working, I am going to get out of here. I said to myself, the next time that he speaks in tongues I am just going to mimic him and pretend that I have the Holy Ghost so I can leave. He then spoke in tongues. Then I went to mimic him. The next thing I knew, I was speaking in a language that sounded like Hebrew, before the audience of people in the Church, motioning my hands like I was before them teaching them something. Then I said to myself, what in the world am I doing. This was totally unlike me. Then the Apostle said, you have been filled with the Holy Ghost. Then all of a sudden I stop speaking this Hebrew like language. The Apostle just kept saying you have been filled with the Holy Ghost. I was saying to myself, is this what it is to be filled with the Holy

Ghost? I did not know what to say. I did not know what to think. I went and sat back down in the same place that I was sitting before. By this time, it was time for the taping of the radio broadcast. As I sat there, Satan began to talk to me. He told me that I did not have the Holy Ghost. He said that as evil as I had been, that God would not give me the Holy Ghost. Satan then brought up to me every evil thing that I had done. He kept saying, you do not have the Holy Ghost. This went on for about an hour as I sat there. After the taping was over and I left the Church, Satan kept up his accusations and saying that I did not have the Holy Ghost. All the way as I drove home, he kept it up. When I entered into my house I said to God that if I received the Holy Ghost, let me know without a shadow of doubt. Immediately I began to speak in tongues. I was speaking loud in tongues. I began to analyze this speaking. I was not trying to mimic. My mouth and tongue were moving and I was not trying to make them move. I was speaking sounding eloquently, whatever I was speaking. This speaking went on for about an hour with me analyzing to see whether it was me or God speaking. I then thought that I might not be able to stop speaking in tongues. Immediately I stop speaking in tongues and God spoke to me clearly and said that my name had been written in the Book of Life and everything has been worth it. I knew what God meant by worth it and I started crying. All of these months. All of these weeks. All of these days. All of the praying. All of the crying. All of this seeking for the Holy Ghost, but it is worth it. Later on I would get baptized by the Apostle in the name of Jesus Christ for the remission of my sins.

This one thing I want to point out. I could have received the Holy Ghost, all the way back in October of 1985, if I had got rid of that dope and the other things of sin. You cannot hold on to the past, anything of the past that is sin, and receive the Holy Ghost. Satan would have caused me to go to hell over (2) two marijuana joints. Two joints would have kept me from immortality.

PROPHETESS SYLVIA FRANKLIN'S TESTIMONIES OF RECEIVING THE HOLY GHOST

When my wife, Prophetess Sylvia Franklin, was a child she had a very depressing life. There was constant arguing and fighting between her father and mother. Her father would be drunk and pull out a gun and threaten to kill her mother and even at certain times to kill her and her brother.

At (10) ten years old, Sylvia would look out of her window and look up and ask God to take away the gloom and let the sun shine. She always would do this. It always seemed to be so gloomy in those days. As time went by in this constant state of family turmoil, at (13) thirteen years old, God did let the sun shine in Sylvia's life. After Sylvia, her mother and brother started attending a small Holiness Church, Sylvia was involved with a street meeting service. This was Apostle William Tumlin's Church. During the meeting the people were singing and praising the Lord. Sylvia then started singing and praising the Lord and all of a sudden she started speaking in tongues.

Not really understanding what had happened to her, Sylvia was in and out of Church. As time passed Sylvia lost the Holy Ghost. At (17) seventeen years old Sylvia was in a service at Apostle William A. Tumlin's Church, All Nations Church of God. While singing and praising was taking place in the Church, Apostle Tumlin came to where Sylvia was and laid hands on her head and she started speaking in tongues. She was restored in the Holy Ghost. Later on she got baptized by Apostle Tumlin in the name of Jesus Christ for the remission of sins. Sylvia's life was never the same again.

OUR OLDEST CHILD ELIJAH JEREMIAH EZEKIEL FRANKLIN'S TESTIMONY OF RECEIVING THE HOLY GHOST

On January 31, 1995 our son, Elijah Jeremiah Ezekiel Franklin, had his fifth birthday. This is the same child the doctors said would have only a ten percent or less chance of being born. This is the same child some would have recommended being aborted (murdered in the womb). This is the same child who is in very good health. This is the same child the doctors said would have probable extreme health problems. This is the same child who was born premature.

After turning five years old, two days later on February 2, 1995, while we (Frederick and

Sylvia) were praying for him in our house during our weekly Thursday night prayer service, he was filled with the Holy Ghost. He spoke in tongues for about an hour. After he finished speaking in tongues, we baptized him in the name of Jesus.

Through the testimony of Elijah's salvation, other children have desired to be saved and were indeed filled with the Holy Ghost and baptized in the name of Jesus.

<u>NOTE THIS</u>. Two Days After Elijah Spoke In Tongues, He Prophesied And Said, God Is Saying To Him, That We Would Be Moving To A Farm In Mobile, With Farm Animals. Later On That Year, In October, We Moved To That Farm.

DANIEL ISAIAH FRANKLIN AND REBEKAH ANNA FRANKLIN'S TESTIMONIES OF RECEIVING THE HOLY GHOST

This dedication is to give praise and glory to God Almighty, Father Jesus our Lord and Savior and to his Son Jesus Christ of whom the Father dwelled in on this earth, for the born again experience of Daniel Isaiah and Rebekah Anna.

June 15, 1998 was a special day in our family. This is the day that we completed household salvation in our family, the day that we could say that all five of us were born again. On this day, June 15, 1998, as we all prayed fervently during our daily dedicated afternoon prayer, God moved mightily in our presence. We were already excited for the young woman that we had prayed to receive the Holy Ghost the past night which we were preparing to baptize after our prayer time.

As we prayed fervently for God to move in a special way that day for the souls to be saved in our community, God spoke to us to pray for Daniel and Rebekah. We, Frederick, Sylvia and Elijah, started praying for them to be filled with the Holy Ghost. As we prayed, we noticed that Daniel and Rebekah were under the influence of the presence of God in praising him and they began to speak in tongues. We wondered could this actually be happening this fast as we had been praying for? Could our five year old son and four year old daughter now finally be filled with the Holy Ghost? We had been praying to God every day since they were conceived in Sylvia's womb for them to receive the Holy Ghost. We didn't really know whether they were speaking in tongues or not at this time because during prayer our children often would mimic us when we were speaking in tongues. But, this time seemed to be different, especially with Rebekah. Daniel Isaiah, every since he was about one year old, always has fervently praised the Lord, singing, dancing, lifting up his hands to God and appearing to speak in tongues. Rebekah, however, did not normally praise God as enthusiastically as did Daniel. But on this day, June 15, 1998, at about 2:00 p.m., our little Rebekah was on fire! And even the normally enthusiastic Daniel seemed to have a double portion. We looked at them and wondered could this actually be it? Could our Daniel Isaiah be filled with the Holy Ghost? Could our son, who was born three months premature, be now born again of the Spirit? Could our son, who at one time only weighed (2) two pounds and (13) thirteen ounces, be born again of the Spirit? Could our son, who the doctors said would have to stay in the hospital for at least three months after he was born, who only stayed one month because he was so healthy, could he actually be speaking in tongues? Could this, our son who is strong and in excellent health who doctors said would have severe and numerous health problems, be born again of the Spirit? Could it also be that our little Rebekah be born again of the Spirit? Could it be that the Daddy's little girl, that he calls "Pretty Pretty" be born again of the Spirit? Could both Daniel Isaiah and Rebekah be filled with the Holy Ghost? Could Frederick now release our second book for publication after waiting for Daniel and Rebekah to be born again so he could dedicate some pages in the book to their born again experience as he had done in our first with Elijah?

We did not want to make a mistake here and tell Daniel and Rebekah that they had been filled with the Holy Ghost, it was too important. We had to be sure. So, we prayed to God for him to tell us clearly whether they had been filled with the Holy Ghost or not.

God answered us quickly and said yes. We were exceedingly glad and satisfied. But, to our shame and astonishment, God also said that Daniel had been filled with the Holy Ghost before now. God did not tell us when, neither did we know. We suspected it was during one of our weekly Thursday night prayer services or during one of our three daily prayer times. God would later let us know that Daniel had received the Holy Ghost when he was (3) three years old during one of our weekly night services. Although we were shamed and rightly so, for not knowing our son was already filled with the Holy Ghost, our joy was rekindled and we went immediately and baptized Daniel Isaiah and Rebekah Anna in the name of Jesus for the remission of their sins to complete their born again experience.

REASONS TO WANT TO BE SAVED

Why would you want to be saved? Well, I will give you three good reasons to want to be saved. You might say, I don't need to be saved. You might say, I'm doing just fine like I am. Well, you might have an argument if you could guarantee the future would be what you want it to be. You might have an argument if you could guarantee that you will be living next year. You might have an argument if you could guarantee that you will be living next month. You might have an argument if you could guarantee that you will be living next week. You might have an argument if you could guarantee that you will be living tomorrow. You might have an argument if you could guarantee you will not die today. You might have an argument if you could guarantee that you will not die the next hour. You might have an argument if you can ensure that you will be living the next five minutes. If you had control over your time of life, you might not need Jesus' salvation. But, since Jesus, the God Almighty, has control over your appointed time of life, if you are not totally stupid, then you should realize that you need to be saved.

This is the bottom line, either ignorance or stupidity causes you not to get saved. Jesus, the God Almighty, before the world was created, assigned an appointed time for each of us to be born. He, also, set the exact time of our death. Jesus has assigned us our parking meter of life. Who is familiar with a prepaid cell phone? Well, for a prepaid cell phone, you have an allotted amount of minutes to use your cell phone. Once you have used all of your minutes, it is useless. It is dead. Well, Jesus, the God Almighty, has assigned us our prepaid cell phone of life. Do you know how many minutes you have left? Supposed you have (15) fifteen minutes left. Suppose (10) ten. Suppose (5) five. Do you know whether an earthquake will now occur at this place or not? Do you know whether an airplane will now or not crash into this building? Do you know whether a terrorist will now or not blow up this building? Jesus knows. Do you know whether you will or will not fall dead in this minute of a heart attack? Do you know on the way from here whether you will have an head on collision with another vehicle and be killed? Jesus knows. Your time clock of life is running out!

The number one trick of Satan is to convince those that are not saved, who want to be saved, that you have more time, until your parking meter of life expires. He hopes to convince you that you have more time, until your prepaid cell phone of life is used up.

You might be one of the fools that might say, that you do not care whether you die without being saved. If this is you, you are indeed a fool. One of the main reasons to get saved is to stay out of hell. If you are one of the ones that say you do not care whether you die without being saved, then you probably do not understand that there is a hell with a wide opened mouth waiting to swallow you. Hell is a real place. When death occurs, you, the real you, your soul, will either go to hell or heaven. If you are saved, you go to heaven. If you are not saved, you go to hell. What is hell, you might ask? Hell is a place where souls are tormented with fire. A very, very, very, hot fire. The hottest fire that we can make on earth, spirits can touch it, walk in, lay on, etc., without it burning them. Spirits are beings that include angels and devils. God, also, is a spirit. Hell is so hot that it burns spirits. Not God, but other Spirits. A person's soul is spirit. A person's soul is the person's desire, feeling, emotions, mind, hearing, sight, taste, smell and memory. The real person. The real you. The body dies and rots. The soul is eternal. It will live either in hell or with God, forever and ever more. Hell is a place located in the center of the earth. Those that are in hell are in continual torment. They are burning continually. There is no relief. Just continual screaming and burning. No rest day nor night. There is no water. There is no air conditioner. There is no fan. There is no kind of cooling. Remember, understand, that they have their feelings in hell. Remember, understand, that they have their desires in hell. Their desire to quench their thirst can never be satisfied. Their desire to alter their circumstances can never be done. Their desire to leave hell will never be fulfilled. They will be in their forever. Their cry out to God for help will be in vain. Hopelessness! Hopelessness! Hopelessness! Pain of burning continually. The pain from a burning fire, if not the worst, is one of the worse pains that you can have. Pains on your hands. Pains on your feet. Pains on your arms. Pains on your legs. Pains on your back. Pains on your belly. Pains on your chest. Pains on your face. Pains on your ears. Pains on your tongue. Pains on the top of your head. Pain everywhere. Pains all the time. All day and all night forever and ever and ever and ever and evermore. They had an alternative, they had another choice, they could have gotten saved.

This is the second good reason to want to get saved. For those of you that believe that there is a God, then you should want to be saved for your love to God. You know that God is a good God, the good God. You know that God has been good to you. You cannot live without God. You cannot walk without God. You cannot talk without God. You cannot eat without God. You cannot sleep without God. You cannot love without God. You cannot be loved without God. You cannot breathe without God. All of these things and many, many, other good things God provides you. And, not only you, but all others even his enemies. Even those that curse him. Even those who prefer to serve Satan rather than God himself. It was God who protected you from death. It was Satan who tried to kill you. It was God who healed you. It was Satan that made you sick. It was Satan who killed your love ones. It was God who protected your love ones from Satan that allowed them to live as long as they did.

To get saved is to show your love and gratitude to God. To get saved is to show your love and gratitude to God for a price that he paid for your salvation. The price was very great. God allowed his Son Jesus of Nazareth to die. There have been some men who have allowed their sons to die for what they considered a good cause or for a friend. God allowed his son to die for his enemies. God, even, allowed his Son to suffer for his enemies. To suffer such suffering never suffered before. Unbearable sufferings. God allowed him to be slapped. God allowed him to be spit on. God allowed his beard to be pulled off of his face, causing pain and bleeding and swelling. God allowed a crown made of thorns to be put on his head. Shoved into his scalp and forehead, causing pain, bleeding and swelling. God allowed his Son to be beat with (39) thirty-nine strokes of a whip that would snatch the meat off his bones. Pain, excruciating pain, bleeding and swelling. God allowed him to be nailed on a tree in his hands and feet, causing pain, excruciating pain, bleeding and swelling. God saw his son suffer. He saw his body bleed, from the top of his head to the bottom of his feet. God saw his Son's body swell, from the top of his head to the bottom of his feet. God saw his Son's body from the top of his head to the bottom of his feet change to a painful black and blue-like color with pain and red with blood. He saw him agonize in pain and misery, until through the bleeding and swelling he was not recognizable as a man. We would not and could not allow our sons and daughters, who we loved, to suffer even for a friend, let along their enemies. All that God has done for us, so much, and He only requires for a token of love, for us to accept his glorious salvation. For us to stay out of hell. So, for those who believe that there is a God, God Almighty, then our love for God should make us want to be saved.

To get saved is to show that God's sacrifice of His Son was not in vain with us. This salvation of ours makes God's investment yield a return. So great investment for such a little return. Without your salvation the little return is even smaller. Just think, by getting saved, the God that created the universe will allow us to be with him for ever and ever more. It will not be just any existence, but God has promised us in the Holy Bible, that we will have no more sorrow, no more pain, no more crying and no more death. I believe that God has allowed me to experience how it will be in heaven. Not long after I was filled with the Holy Ghost, while living in Montgomery, Alabama, God gave me a visitation. While sitting in my bed, with my legs and my feet in the bed, eyes wide opened, the presence, the glory, the anointing of God, moved on me. I felt it. I knew somehow it was God. I don't know how I knew, but I knew without a shadow of doubt that it was God. The sensation, the feeling, started at the bottom of my feet. It then covered my feet. It proceeded up my legs. It continued up my body. It covered my thighs. It just continued to go up my body. It covered my belly and chest. Then it went in my shoulders and through my arms, hands and fingers. It went up my neck and covered my head. It was all over me. Let me try to tell you how it felt. Words cannot properly explain how good it felt. This felt at least a hundred times better than the best feeling I have ever had. There is nothing we have experience to compare with it. Let me tell you this. Everything on me felt good. My fingernails, even, felt good. My hair, even, felt good. Even each strand of hair felt good. It felt so good until I started asking God to allow those that I knew to experience it. I started calling out their names for God to allow them to feel it. I mentioned my mother, brother, sisters, grandmother, nieces, nephews, aunts, uncles, first cousins, second cousins, other relatives, friends, co-workers, college classmates that were friends, church members and maybe some others, for God to allow to experience what I was feeling. I don't know the exact time, this feeling, this presence, this anointing, this visitation, lasted. It was a long time. Maybe an hour or longer. I believe God allowed me to experience what heaven feels like. People, if this is what heaven feels like, this along is worth getting saved for.

Now I will address the third good reason to get saved. If you are one who thinks that to be saved has no present life benefit, consider this. Soon in these days, there will be a great tormenting plague to cover the whole earth. This will happen very soon. Possibly, during George W. Bush's time as President. This torment will be excruciating pain. This pain will be continual. It will affect all ages, babies, young children, teenagers, young adults, middle age adults, senior citizens, all. The pain of this plague will be so horrible, until the people will want to die. People will want to commit suicide. There will be no medicine for cure. There will be no medicine for relief. There will be screaming all over the earth. The children will be screaming. The parents will be screaming. The grandparents will be screaming. The great grandparents will be screaming. The nurses will be screaming. The doctors will be screaming. Those of the police force will be screaming. Those of the army will be screaming. Those of the Air Force will be screaming. Those of the Navy will be screaming. Those of the Marines will be screaming. The members of the House of Representatives will be screaming. The Senators will be screaming. The Supreme Court Justices will be screaming. The Vice President will be screaming. The President will be screaming. The Pope will scream. All will scream!

All of this paining. All of this misery. All of this hurting and no relief. No relief for five months. Yes! It will last for (5) five months. And think about this. It is hard to get sleep when you are in pain. What hopelessness. The curse of this plague will be so bad that people will want to die. However, the curse of this plague will not allow them to die. This curse has been told about in the Book of Revelation of the Holy Bible. Turn to the Book of Revelation in your Bible. Look at Chapter (9) Nine. Read Verse (6) Six.

Revelation Ch.9, V.6
"And in those days shall men seek death, and shall not find it; and shall desire to die and death shall flee from them."

This great excruciating painful plague will soon happen. This painful plague will be the closest thing to hell itself. It will be so horrible, so excruciating, that God told me to write a book about it to warn the people. This is the book here. The name is "Five Month Desire To Die, But Not Possible When Fifth Angel Blows Trumpet." The only ones on planet Earth that will not be affected with this great painful plague, will be those that have the Holy Ghost. You must have the Holy Ghost to be saved. All that have the Holy Ghost speak in tongues.

If you, yet, after reading this, due to some custom, tradition or religion, do not get saved, it is because you are too stupid to get saved.

THE FOUR EASY STEPS TO GET SAVED/BORN AGAIN:

1. Repent:

   a. ask God to forgive your sins, ask in the name of Jesus;
   b. surrender your will for God's will to be done in your life.

2. Ask God to save you, to fill you with the Holy Ghost, ask in the name of Jesus.

3. Do not ask God anymore to save you, just thank God, praise God for saving you. You must thank God in the name of Jesus. At the point of your greatest sincerity, you will speak in another language. This will be your sign of confirmation. God will be using your mouth to speak a language spoken somewhere on earth that you have not learned. This is your sign that you are born of the Spirit.

4. Get baptized in the name of Jesus Christ.

John Ch.3,Vs.3&5

"Jesus answered . . . Except a man be born again, he cannot see the kingdom of God . . . Jesus answered . . . Except a man be born of water and of the Spirit he cannot enter into the kingdom of God."

John Ch.3,V.8

". . . thou hearest the sound thereof . . . so is everyone that is born of the Spirit."

Colossians Ch.3,V.17

"And whatsoever ye do in word or deed, do all in the name of the Lord Jesus . . ."

LIST OF BOOKS THAT WE HAVE WRITTEN

1. Proof That **YOUR LEADERS** Have **DECEIVED YOU** And The End Times

2. What **GOD** Is Now Telling His Prophets **ABOUT** The **END TIMES**

3. Five Month **DESIRE TO DIE**, But Not Possible When Fifth Angel Blows Trumpet

4. **GOD's** Word Concern **MARRIAGE AND DIVORCE**

5. The Name Of The (Anti-Christ) Beast And **666** Identification

6. **WHERE GOD's PEOPLE** (Saints) **GO** When GOD Comes Back To Get Us

7. How You Can **PROVE** That **YOU HAVE** A **SOUL**

18. The **NAME OF** The **(ANTI-CHRIST) BEAST**

19. **WHO IS** The **(FALSE PROPHET)** Second Beast

20. **WHY, WHEN** And **HOW** The (Anti-Christ) Beast **WILL DECEIVE** The World That **HE IS GOD**

21. The **TEN HORNS** Of The Books Of **DANIEL** And **REVELATION**

22. **UNDERSTANDING** The **BOOK OF** Revelation To Understand the Book Of **REVELATION**

23. Main Arguments For The **RAPTURE** Being **BEFORE** The **GREAT TRIBULATION** And Why They Are **NOT TRUE**

24. **MAKING SATAN** And His Kingdom **PAY** A Big Price **SO** The **END CAN COME**

25. Makeup, Membership And Money Of **GOD'S CHURCH** And **HOW GOD WANTS** Them To Be

35. **GOD'S FOUR** Healings And Deliverances Which He **DESIRES FOR US**

36. The Parallel/Comparison Of **JEWS AND BLACK PEOPLE** Of The United States

37. The **CHRONOLOGICAL ACCOUNT** Of The Gospels Of What Is Said **ABOUT JESUS**

38. **TIMES** That **GOD APPEARED UNTO US**

39. The **WHOLE WORLD** Becoming **AS SODOM**

40. The **TWO** Main **REASONS CMMUNION** Is To Be **TAKEN**

41. The **DOOR IS CLOSING ON** The Last Opportunity For **IMMORTALITY**

42. **(CONFIDENTIAL—(ONLY FOR THE 15 APOSTLE)—"APOSTLES HANDBOOK** Of Ministry Tasks Before & During The Great Tribulation")

43. **WORDS FROM GOD**, By God Appearing To Us Or Just Talking To Us, **FOR THE END TIMES**

44. **GOD SAID BLACK PEOPLE** In The United States **ARE JEWS**.

45. **GOD** Tells How To **ELIMINATE FAMINE**

46. What Was **CAIN'S MARK?**

47. **THE FINAL EXODUS**

HOW TO GET SAVED

To Be Saved You must Speak with Tongues & Be Baptized in the Name of Jesus

<u>John Ch. 3, V. 3</u>
"Jesus answered . . . Except a man be born again, he cannot see the Kingdom of God."

<u>John Ch. 3, V. 5</u>
"Jesus answered . . . Except a man be born of water and of the Spirit, he cannot enter into the Kingdom of God."

<u>Acts Ch. 2, V. 38</u>
". . . Repent, and be baptized every one of you in the name of Jesus Christ for the remission of sins, and ye shall receive the gift of the Holy Ghost."

<u>How to Repent</u>: (1) Sincerely ask God to forgive your sins, ask in the name of Jesus; (2) Surrender your will for God's Will to be done in your life.

<u>After Repenting</u>: Sincerely ask God to save you, to give you his Spirit, to give you the Holy Ghost, to have you to speak with other tongues. [Once you have asked, then just continue to thank God for doing so, just praise him, sincerely. You WILL then speak in tongues.]

<u>John Ch. 3, V. 8</u>
". . . thou hearest the sound thereof . . . so is everyone that is born of the Spirit."

<u>After Speaking in Tongues</u>: Get baptized in the name of Jesus, again you must be repented.

<u>NOTE</u>: You can be baptized and then receive the Holy Ghost or be filled with the Holy Ghost then be baptized.

<u>Speaking in Tongues</u>: Speaking in tongues (unknown language) is God speaking through you.

<u>Mark Ch. 16, V. 17</u>
"And these signs shall follow them that believe . . . they shall speak with new tongues."

<u>Acts Ch. 2, V. 4</u>
". . . and began to speak with other tongues as the Spirit gave them utterance."

<u>Acts Ch. 22, V 16</u>
". . . be baptized, and wash away thy sins . . ."

<u>Colossians Ch. 3, V. 17</u>
"And whatsoever ye do in word or deed, do all in the name of the Lord Jesus . . ."

The name of the Father is Jesus, the name of the Son is Jesus, the name of the Holy Ghost is Jesus.

<u>John Ch. 17, V. 26</u>
"And I have declared thy name unto them . . ."

<u>John Ch. 5, V. 43</u>
"I am come in my Father's name . . ."

<u>Hebrews Ch. 1, V. 4</u>
". . . he hath by inheritance obtained a more excellent name . . ."

John Ch. 4, V. 24
"God is a Spirit . . ."

Question: Is the Father Holy? Answer: Yes. God is a Father; God was manifested in flesh as a Son; God is a Spirit, the Holy Spirit, the Holy Ghost.

I, Frederick E. Franklin, am a Father, am a Son, am a Human Being. Father, Son, Holy Ghost and Father, Son, Human Being are titles. God's name is Jesus.

Matthew Ch. 28, V. 19
". . . Teach all nations, baptizing them in the name of . . . the Son . . ."

TO BE A PART OF THE F&SF MINISTRY FOR JESUS THE FOLLOWING WILL BE EXPECTED

II Timothy Ch.2, V.3

"Thou therefore endure hardness, as a good soldier of Jesus Christ."

Ephesians Ch.6, V.10

". . . be strong in the Lord, and in the power of his might."

Ephesians Ch.5, V.27

"That he might present it to himself a glorious church, not having spot, or wrinkle, or any such thing; but that it should be holy and without blemish."

The F&SF Ministry For JESUS Soldier Will:

1. Be Filled With The Holy Ghost (Evidenced By Speaking In Tongues)
2. Be Baptized In The Name Of JESUS
3. Be Honest And Sincere
4. ave Love And Compassion For Others
5. Properly Pay Tithes And Give Offerings
6. elieve In One God (The God Of Abraham, Isaac, And Jacob)
7. Worship Only God Almighty, The Creator Of The Universe, JESUS
8. Be Holy
9. Attend Sabbath (Friday Dark To Saturday Dark) Service(s)
10. Attend Other Service(s) When Possible
11. Make Continuous Sincere Efforts For Souls To Be Saved
12. Profess/Testify That You Must Speak In Tongues And Be Baptized In The Name Of Jesus To Be Saved
13. Profess/Testify That The Great Tribulation Is Before The Rapture
14. Reveal That Pope John Paul II Is The (Anti-Christ) Beast
15. Be Bold (Not A Coward)

16. Desire To Grow In Revelation And Power Of God

17. Be Faithful And Dedicated To The F&SF Ministry For JESUS

18. Receive/Accept The Teachings Of Apostle Frederick E. Franklin

19. Not Espouse Teachings/Doctrines Contrary To That Of Apostle Frederick E. Franklin

20. Adhere To The Leadership Of Apostle Frederick E. Franklin

21. Not Be A Liar

22. Not Be A Hypocrite

23. Not Be A Witchcraft Worker

24. Not Be A Partaker Of Idolatry.

EXCERPTS FROM OUR BOOK "THE NAME OF THE (ANTI-CHRIST) BEAST AND 666 IDENTIFICATION"

There will be great deception. The scriptures indicate that the (Anti-Christ) Beast, Pope John Paul II, Carol Josef Wojtyla, will fake his death. Later on, to fake being resurrected from the dead. All to the end, to fake that he is God. All to the end, to discredit JESUS' resurrection. All to the end, to discredit that JESUS is God and rather to show/deceive that he is God.

Revelation Ch. 17, V. 8
". . . the beast that was, and is not, and yet is."

The Above scripture indicates that the Beast, Pope John Paul II, Carol Josef Wojtyla, was living. It further indicates that he will seem not to be living, but he actually will be living. He was living. He appears not to be living. But, he yet is living.

JESUS IS GOD

1. <u>I John Chapter 5, Verse 20</u>
"And we know that the Son of God is come, and hath given us an understanding, that we may know him that is true, and we are in him that is true, even in his Son Jesus Christ. This is the true God, and eternal life."

2. <u>John Chapter 1, Verses 1 & 14</u>
"In the beginning was the Word, and the Word was with God, and the Word was God. And the Word was made flesh, and dwelt among us, (and we beheld his glory, the glory as of the only begotten of the Father,) full of grace and truth."

3. <u>I Timothy Chapter 3, Verse 16</u>
"And without controversy great is the mystery of godliness: God was manifest in the flesh, justified in the Spirit, seen of angels, preached unto the Gentiles, believed on in the world, received up into glory."

4. Isaiah Chapter 9, Verse 6

"For unto us a child is born, unto us a son is given: and the government shall be upon his shoulder: and his name shall be called Wonderful, Counsellor, The mighty God, The everlasting Father, The Prince of Peace."

5. Matthew Chapter 1, Verse 23

"Behold, a virgin shall be with child, and shall bring forth a son, and they shall call his name Emmanuel, which being interpreted is, God with us."

6. Titus Chapter 1, Verses 3 & 4

". . . God our Saviour; . . . the Lord Jesus Christ our Saviour."

7. Isaiah Chapter 43, Verse 11

"I, even I, am the Lord; and beside me there is no Saviour."

8. Isaiah Chapter 44, Verse 6

"Thus saith the Lord the King of Israel, and his redeemer the Lord of hosts; I am the first, and I am the last; and beside me there is no God."

9. Revelation Chapter 1, Verses 17 & 18
". . . I am the first and the last: I am he that liveth, and was dead . . ."

10. Revelation Chapter 22, Verses 13 & 16
"I am Alpha and Omega, the beginning and the end, the first and the last. I Jesus have sent mine angel to testify unto you these things in the churches . . ."

11. Isaiah Chapter 44, Verse 24
"Thus saith the Lord, thy redeemer, and he that formed thee from the womb, I am the Lord that maketh all things; that stretcheth forth the heavens alone; that spreadeth abroad the earth by myself . . ."

12. Colossians Chapter 1, Verses 16, 17 & 18
"For by him were all things created, that are in heaven, and that are in earth, visible and invisible, whether they be thrones, or powers: all things were created by him, and for him: And he is before all things, and by him all things consist. And he is the head of the body the church."

13. <u>Ephesians Chapter 5, Verse 23</u>
"For the husband is the head of the wife, even as Christ is the head of the church: and he is the saviour of the body."

14. <u>Colossians Chapter 2, Verse 9</u>
"For in Him dwelleth all the fullness of the Godhead bodily."

15. <u>I John Chapter 5, Verse 7</u>
". . . three that bear record in heaven, the Father, the Word, and the Holy Ghost: and these three are one."

16. <u>Revelation Chapter 15, Verse 3</u>
". . . Great and Marvelous are thy works, Lord God Almighty; just and true are thy ways, thou King of saints."

17. <u>Revelation Chapter 17, Verse 14</u>
". . . and the Lamb shall overcome them: for he is Lord of lords, and King of kings; and they that are with him are called, and chosen, and faithful."

18. <u>I Thessalonians Chapter 3, Verse 13</u>

". . . God, even our Father, at the coming of our Lord Jesus Christ with all his saints."

19. <u>Zechariah Chapter 14, Verse 5</u>

". . . and the Lord my God shall come, and all the saints with thee."

20. <u>I John Chapter 3, Verse 16</u>

"Hereby perceive we the love of God, because he laid down his life for us."

21. Etc.

<u>THE FOUR EASY STEPS TO GET SAVED/BORN AGAIN</u>:

1. Repent:

   a. ask God to forgive your sins, ask in the name of Jesus;
   b. surrender your will for God's will to be done in your life.

2. Ask God to save you, to fill you with the Holy Ghost, ask in the name of Jesus.

3. Do not ask God anymore to save you, just thank God, praise God for saving you. You must thank God in the name of Jesus. At the point of your greatest sincerity, you will speak in another language. This will be your sign of confirmation. God will be using your mouth to speak a language spoken somewhere on earth that you have not learned. This is your sign that you are born of the Spirit.

4. Get baptized in the name of Jesus Christ.

John Ch.3,Vs.3&5

"Jesus answered . . . Except a man be born again, he cannot see the kingdom of God . . . Jesus answered . . . Except a man be born of water and of the Spirit he cannot enter into the kingdom of God."

John Ch.3,V.8

". . . thou hearest the sound thereof . . . so is everyone that is born of the Spirit."

Colossians Ch.3,V.17

"And whatsoever ye do in word or deed, do all in the name of the Lord Jesus . . ."

THE SABBATH

What Is The Sabbath?

The Sabbath is a holy day ordained by God to be so. It is a day for all to cease from work.

When Is The Sabbath?

The Sabbath is the last day, the seventh day of the week.

Genesis Ch.2, Vs. 1-3
"Thus the heavens and earth were finished, and all of the host of them. And on the seventh day God ended his work which he had made; and he rested on the seventh day from all his work which he had made."

Exodus Ch.20, Vs. 8-11
"Remember the sabbath day, to keep it holy. Six days shalt thou labour, and do all thy work: But the seventh day is the sabbath of the Lord

thy God: in it thou shalt not do any work, thou, nor thy son, nor thy daughter, thy manservant, nor thy cattle, nor thy stranger that is within thy gates: For in six days the Lord made heaven and earth, the sea, and all that in them is, and rested the seventh day: wherefore the Lord blessed the sabbath day, and hallowed it."

Exodus Ch.23, V. 12
"Six days thou shalt do thy work, and on the seventh day thou shalt rest: that thine ox and thine ass may rest, and the son of thy handmaid, and the stranger, may be refreshed."

When Does The Day Start?

The day starts at dark and goes to the next day at dark.

Genesis Ch.1, Vs 5, 8, 13, 19, 23 & 31
". . . And the evening and the morning were the first day . . . And the evening and the morning were the second day. And the evening and the morning were the third day. And the evening and the morning were the fourth day. And the evening and the morning were the fifth day.

And God saw every thing that he had made and, behold, it was very good. And the evening and the morning were the sixth day."

Is It A Sin To NOT Keep Or Violate The Sabbath?

To keep the Sabbath is one of the ten commandments. One of the ten commandments say thou shalt not kill. Another says thou shalt not steal. Just as it is sin to kill and steal, likewise, is it a sin to NOT keep or to violate the Sabbath.

Exodus Ch.20, V. 13-15
"Thou shalt not kill. Thou shalt not commit adultery. Thou shalt not steal."

What You Should Not Do On The Sabbath.

Exodus Ch.20, V. 10
"But the seventh day is the sabbath of the Lord thy God: in it thou shalt not do any work, thou, nor thy son, nor thy daughter, thy manservant, nor thy maidservant, nor thy cattle, nor thy stranger that is within thy gates . . ."

<u>Nehemiah Ch.10, V. 31</u>

"And if the people of the land bring ware or any victuals on the sabbath day to sell, that we would not buy it of them on the sabbath, or on the holy day . . ."

<u>Nehemiah Ch.13, Vs. 16-18</u>

"There dwelt men of Tyre also therein, which brought fish, and all manner of ware, and sold on the sabbath unto the children of Judah, and in Jerusalem. Then I contended with nobles of Judah, and said unto them, What evil thing is this that ye do, and profane the sabbath day? Did not your fathers thus, and did not our God bring all this wrath upon this city? Yet ye bring more wrath upon Israel by profaning the sabbath."

What Happened When The Sabbath Was Not Kept Or Violated Intentionally.

<u>Numbers Ch.15, Vs. 32-36</u>

"And while the children of Israel were in the wilderness, they found a man that gathered sticks upon the sabbath day. And they that found him gathering sticks brought him unto

Moses and Aaron and unto all the congregation. And they put him in ward, because it was not declared what should be done unto him. And the Lord said unto Moses, The man shall be surely put to death: all the congregation shall stone him with stones without the camp. And all the congregation brought him without the camp, and stone with stones and he died; as the Lord commanded Moses."

Numbers Ch.15, Vs. 30-31
"But the soul that doeth ought presumptuously, whether he be born in the land, or a stranger, the same reproacheth the Lord; and that soul shall be cut off from among his people. Because he hath despised the word of the Lord, and hath broken his commandment, that soul shall be utterly cut off; his iniquity shall be upon."

Not Keeping Or Violating The Sabbath Out Of Ignorance.

Numbers Ch.15, Vs. 27-28
"And if any soul sin through ignorance . . . the priest shall make atonement for the soul that sinneth ignorantly, when he sinneth by

ignorance before the Lord, to make atonement for him; and it shall be forgiven him."

Numbers Ch.15, Vs. 22, 24-25
"And if ye erred, and not observed at all these commandments . . . Then if it shall be, if ought be committed by ignorance without the knowledge . . . the priest shall make an atonement for all the congregation of the children of Israel, and it shall be forgiven them . . ."

Other Benefits Of Keeping The Sabbath.

God is pleased with those who obey his word and the promises of the Holy Bible is available to you.

Isaiah Ch.56 Vs. 2, 5-7
"Blessed is the man that doeth this, and the son of man that layeth hold on it; that keepeth the sabbath from polluting it, and keep his hand from doing any evil. Even unto them will I give in mine house and within my walls a place and a name better than the sons and daughters. I will give them an everlasting name, that shall

not be cut off. Also the sons of the stranger that join themselves to the Lord, to serve him, and to love the name of the Lord, to be his servants, every one that keepeth the sabbath from polluting it, and taketh hold of my covenant; Even them will I bring unto my holy mountain, and make them joyful in my house of prayer . . . their sacrifices shall be accepted upon mine altar; for mine house shall be called an house of prayer for all people."

Exodus Ch.23, V. 12
". . . thou shalt rest . . . be refreshed."

Exodus Ch.20, V.12
". . . the Lord blessed the sabbath day, and hallowed it."

Why Has Sunday Been Chosen As The So-Called Sabbath By The So-Called Christians And Some Christians?

The Pope of 325 A.D. birth this blasphemy of changing the Sabbath day from the seventh day to the first day of the week. This blasphemous change of the sabbath to Sunday was done to have the people worship God the Almighty on the same day as the worship of the sun god. Sunday the worship of the Sun god. This blasphemous change was prophesied of in the scriptures.

Matthew Ch.24, V. 24
"For there shall arise false Christs, and false prophets, and shall shew great signs and wonders; insomuch that, if it were possible, they shall deceive the very elect."

Daniel Ch.7, V. 25
"And he shall speak great words against the most High, and shall wear out the saints of the most High, and think to change times and laws . . ."

Daniel Ch.8, V. 12
"An host was given him against the daily sacrifice by reason of transgression, and it cast down the truth to the ground; and it practiced and prospered."

To justify this blasphemous change, he, the Pope, had to use scriptures of the Holy Bible. He used three places in the scriptures.

Matthew Ch.28, Vs. 1-6

"In the end of the sabbath, as it began to dawn toward the first day of the week, came Mary Magdalene and the other Mary to see the sepulchre. And, behold, there was a great earthquake: for the angel of Lord descended from heaven, and came and rolled back the stone from the door, and sat upon it. His countenance was like lightning, and his raiment white as snow; And for fear of him the keepers did shake, and became as dead men. And the angel answered and said unto the women, Fear ye not: for I know that ye seek Jesus, which was crucified. He is not here: for he is risen, as he said. Come, see the place where the Lord lay."

Supposedly, because Jesus was resurrected on the first day of the week, the sabbath should be changed to the first day of the week.

I Corinthians Ch.16, Vs. 1-3

"Now concerning the collection for the saints, as I have given order to the churches of Galatia, even so do ye. Upon the first day of the week let every one of you lay by him in store, as God hath prospered him, that there be no gatherings when I come. And when I come, whosoever ye shall approve by your letters, them will I send to bring your liberality to Jerusalem."

Supposedly, because Paul told them to take up a collection on the first day of the week, this, therefore, means that the New Testament Church's sabbath is on the first day of the week.

Acts Ch.20, V. 7

"And upon the first day of the week, when the disciples came together to break bread, Paul preached to them, ready to depart on the morrow, and continued his speech until midnight."

Supposedly, because the disciples came together on the first day means that they came to hear the word, and because Paul preached on the first day, supposedly, this shows that the

New Testament Church had as its sabbath the first day of the week.

What ridiculous justification(s) to change the Sabbath to the first day of the week.

Scriptures Of The New Testament Refuting The So-Called Sunday Sabbath.

Let us first look at the Pope's last so-called justification, Acts Ch.20, V. 7. When the scriptures said that they came "together to break bread," it means that they came together to eat. While they were there together, Paul took this opportunity to preached to them. Like any preacher would do. Refer to the immediate following scriptures, Acts Ch.20, Vs. 8-12.

Acts Ch.20, Vs. 8-12

"And there were many lights in the upper chamber, where they were gathered together. And there sat in the window a certain young man named Eutychus, being fallen into a deep sleep: and as Paul was long preaching, he sunk down with sleep, and fell down from the third loft, and was taken up dead. And Paul went down, and fell on him, and embracing him said, Trouble not yourselves; for his life is in him. When he therefore was come up again, and had broken bread, and eaten, and talked a long while, even till break of day, so he departed. And they brought the young man alive, and were not a little comforted."

Let us now look at the Pope's I Corinthians Ch.16, Vs. 1-3, justification. Here Paul tells the Church of Corinth to give an offering to the Church in Jerusalem. He said take up collection on the first day of the week. Note that Paul said that there should not be any gathering. The people could not gather on the sabbath day to sell or give their goods or livestock to get a collection, so Paul said do it on the first day of the week. And whatever they gathered on the first day of the week, that is where their offering would come from.

Let us now look at the Pope's third and remaining justification, Matthew Ch.28, Vs. 1-6. These scriptures speak of Jesus' resurrection on the first day of they week. Somehow, this gives us the right to change God's word of a seventh day Sabbath. This is nonsense. God says that there is nothing above his word, not even the name of Jesus.

Psalm 138, V. 2

"I will worship toward thy holy temple, and praise thy name for thy lovingkindness and for thy truth: for thou hast magnified thy word above all thy name."

Now let us see when Paul, Jews and the Gentiles, the New Testament Church, really worshipped. When their Sabbath actually was.

Acts Ch.18, V. 4

"And he reasoned in the synagogue every Sabbath, and persuaded the Jews and the Greeks"

Acts Ch.13, Vs. 13-17, 22-23, 42-44

"Now when Paul and his company loosed from Paphos . . . they came to Antioch . . . and went into the synagogue on the sabbath day, and sat down. And after the reading of the law and the prophets the rulers of the synagogue sent unto them, saying, Ye men and brethren, if ye have any word of exhortation for the people, say on. Then Paul stood up, and beckoning with his hand said, Men of Israel, and ye that fear God, give audience. The God of this people of Israel chose our fathers . . . he raised up unto them David to be their King . . . Of this man's seed hath God according to his promise raised unto Israel a Savior, Jesus . . . And when the Jews were gone out of the synagogue, the Gentiles besought that these words might be preached to them the next sabbath. Now when the congregation was broken up, many of the Jews and religious proselytes followed Paul . . . And the next sabbath day came almost the whole city together to hear the word of God."

Note: Jews that worshipped God, only worshipped on the seventh day, the real Sabbath day.

<u>I Peter Ch.3, Vs. 15-16</u>
"But sanctify the Lord God in your hearts: and be ready always to give an answer to every man that asketh you a reason of the hope that is in you with meekness and fear: Having a good conscience; that, whereas they speak evil

of you, as of evildoers, they may be ashamed that falsely accuse your good conversation in Christ."

What About Colossians Chapter 2, Verse 16?

<u>Colossians Ch.2, V. 16</u>
Let no man judge you in meat, or in drink, or respect of an holyday, or of the new moon, or of the sabbaths . . ."

· There are more than one kind of sabbath referred to in the Holy Bible. There is the seventh day sabbath as has been discussed thus far and there are other sabbaths and holydays. These other sabbaths and holydays are what is referred to in Colossians Chapter 2, Verse 16. These sabbaths included the Passover, feast days, and some other holydays observed by the Jews. Among these days was The Dedication Of The Temple built by Solomon.

<u>John Ch.10, Vs. 22-23</u>
"And it was at Jerusalem the feast of the dedication, and it was winter. And Jesus walked in the temple in Solomon's porch."

Another such sabbath day is referred to in John Chapter 19, Verse 31.

John Ch.19, V. 31
"The Jews therefore, because it was the preparation, that the bodies should not remain upon the cross on the sabbath day, (for that sabbath was an high day,) . . ."

The lack of understanding of the above scripture is how the Pope of 325 A.D. has been able to deceive the people in celebrating the worship of the Spring goddess. This is the Easter celebration. Refer to our book, "Jesus Was Not Crucified When As Has Been Taught."

Here are some of the scriptures referring to the other sabbaths: Leviticus Ch.19, Vs. 1-3; Leviticus Ch.19, V. 30; Leviticus Ch.16, Vs. 29-31; Leviticus Ch.25, Vs. 1-5; Leviticus Ch.26, Vs. 27-35; Leviticus Ch.23, Vs. 4-7; Leviticus Ch.23, Vs. 15, 21, 23-28, 32-36 & 38-39; I Kings Ch.8, Vs. 63-66; etc.

These are the ordinances that Jesus blotted out, even nailing to them the cross.

SPECIAL EXCEPTIONS TO WORKING ON THE SABBATH:

People who try to get around the word of God concerning not working on the Sabbath, try to use certain instances when JESUS said it was alright to do certain things on the Sabbath. They point to the scriptures when JESUS' disciples were hungry and they plucked corn on the Sabbath. They, also, refer to the scriptures when JESUS healed on the Sabbath; the Pharisees complained that JESUS was working on the Sabbath.

EXPLANATION:

JESUS indicates his justification for the efforts on the Sabbath by two short statements.

1. In The Plucking Of Corn On The Sabbath—
    JESUS says—
    ("The sabbath was made for man, and not man for the sabbath.")
    JESUS does not want or require anyone to starve because it is the Sabbath. Refer to Mark Ch. 2, Vs. 23-28.

<u>Mark Ch. 2, Vs. 23-25&27</u>

"And it came to pass, that he went through the corn fields on the sabbath day: and his disciples began, as they went, to pluck the ears of corn. And the Pharisees said unto him, Behold, why do they on the sabbath day that which is unlawful? And he said unto them, Have ye never read what David did, when he had need, and was a hungred, he, and they that were with him? How he went into the house of God in the days of Abiathar the high priest, and did eat showbread, which is not lawful to eat but for the priest, and gave also to them which were with him? And he said unto them, The sabbath was made for man, and not man for the sabbath.

2. In The Healing On The Sabbath—
   JESUS Indicates—
   (It is right to do good on the sabbath.)
   During the work of God is always permitted, even on the Sabbath. Refer to Luke Ch. 13, Vs. 14,15&16.

<u>Luke Ch. 13, Vs. 14,15&16</u>

"And the ruler of the synagogue answer with indignation, because that Jesus had healed on the Sabbath day, and said unto the people, There are six days in which men ought to work: in them therefore come and be healed, and not sabbath day. The Lord then answered him, and said, Thou hypocrite, doth not each one of you on the sabbath loose his ox or his ass from the stall, and lead him away to watering? And ought not this woman, being a daughter of Abraham, whom Satan hath bound, lo these eighteen years, be loosed from this bond on the sabbath day?"

If there is an emergency or critical need that happens the day of the Sabbath, JESUS does not expect you to ignore it. JESUS does not expect you to let someone suffer or die because it is the Sabbath. This does not include other regularly scheduled jobs or occupations on the Sabbath to meet your family needs. Ministering is always permitted, even on the Sabbath. Except for the above, the work that is not permitted on the Sabbath is work that you do on the six other days of the week.

THE FOUR EASY STEPS TO GET SAVED/BORN AGAIN:

1. Repent:

   a. ask God to forgive your sins, ask in the name of Jesus;
   b. surrender your will for God's will to be done in your life.

2. Ask God to save you, to fill you with the Holy Ghost, ask in the name of Jesus.
3. Do not ask God anymore to save you, just thank God, praise God for saving you. You must thank God in the name of Jesus. At the point of your greatest sincerity, you will speak in another language. This will be your sign of confirmation. God will be using your mouth to speak a language spoken somewhere on earth that you have not learned. This is your sign that you are born of the Spirit.
4. Get baptized in the name of Jesus Christ.

John Ch.3,Vs.3&5

"Jesus answered . . . Except a man be born again, he cannot see the kingdom of God . . . Jesus answered . . . Except a man be born of water and of the Spirit he cannot enter into the kingdom of God."

John Ch.3,V.8

". . . thou hearest the sound thereof . . . so is everyone that is born of the Spirit."

Colossians Ch.3,V.17

"And whatsoever ye do in word or deed, do all in the name of the Lord Jesus . . ."

CONTACT PAGE

We provide this page for those of you who desire to get in contact with us regarding:

I.   Ministering

   A. Preaching
   B. Singing
   C. Being prayed for

II. Ordering tapes

   A. Audio of this book
   B. Preaching
   C. Singing
   D. Additional end times prophecies

III. Ordering books

IV. Questions concerning our next book

V.   Other questions.

Remember to give your address. For a quicker response, provide a telephone number where you can be reached.

Frederick & Sylvia Franklin's
Ministry for JESUS
2669 Meadowview Drive
Mobile, AL, 36695
Telephone #: (251) 644-4329

WHERE TO PURCHASE OUR BOOKS

BY APOSTLE FREDERICK E. FRANKLIN

BOOKSTORE SALES:

(25,000 BOOKSTORES)

1. BARNES & NOBLE
2. BOOKS A MILLION
3. ETC.

INTERNET SALES:

AMAZON.COM

DIRECT SALES:

2669 MEADOWVIEW DR.
MOBILE, ALABAMA 36695
PH. #: (251) 644-4329

ABOUT THE AUTHOR

"JESUS WAS NOT CRUCIFIED WHEN AS HAS BEEN TAUGHT" was written by Apostle Frederick E. Franklin of the ministry of F & SF Ministry For JESUS. What has been written is revelation from God that has been given to Frederick and his wife Sylvia. Frederick E. Franklin is an apostle, prophet and end times preacher. His wife, Sylvia Franklin, is a prophetess, evangelist and singer. The ministry positions stated above are what God, himself, has said/ordained and anointed them to be. Frederick and Sylvia have three children, Elijah Jeremiah Ezekiel Franklin, Daniel Isaiah Franklin, and Rebekah Anna Franklin. Frederick E. Franklin was a successful electrical engineer in private industry, state and federal government and also self-employment, before he was born again and told by God to preach.